Simon Mayor

The Mandolin Tutor

Acoustics

The Mandolin Tutor
Simon Mayor

ISBN 0--9522776-1-1

Third edition 2008

First published in 1995 by
Acoustics (Publishing)
PO Box 350
Reading RG6 7DQ
Berkshire
England
www.AcousticsRecords.co.uk

© Simon Mayor 1995

Design of front and back cover by Caroline Crampton
Layout of front and back cover by John Hedgecock
Illustrations © Hilary James 1995
Front cover photographs © Simon Mayor 1995
Back cover photograph © Nigel Tribbeck 1995
Other photographs © Andy Pegg 1995

It would be wonderful to think there were a mandolin teacher on every street. Such a scene may have existed in Italy in days gone by, but certainly at the time of writing the instrument doesn't enjoy the same popularity as it did then or even as it did during the heyday of the mandolin orchestras in the first half of the 20th century. Popularity goes in waves, though, and in the 21st century there is no doubt that the gods are smiling once again on our little eight-stringed friend.

While the Italians may not have succeeded in maintaining the profile of the mandolin at home, it has become a significant cultural export. The Japanese have adopted the round-back variety and the instrument's classical repertoire with huge enthusiasm. The South Americans have found flat-back mandolins a perfect vehicle for wild Latin rhythms, influenced largely by the exceptional playing of Jacob do Bandolim. In Britain and Ireland the mandolin has a small but dedicated circle of classical players, and is widely used in folk music. The USA has spawned more than its fair share of world class players, thanks in part to the many people of Italian descent but more significantly to the influence of one man, Bill Monroe.

Monroe virtually single-handedly fashioned a new musical style called bluegrass in the 1930s but, more importantly to mandolinists, redefined both the role and the sound of the instrument. There had previously been a tendency to play the mandolin 'prettily', but in Monroe's hands it screamed bluegrass solos, roared through fiddle tunes, and also acted as the band's metronome, chopping off-beat chords to hold the rhythm together.

The last few decades have seen the instrument branch out from this pivotal role in bluegrass into jazz (even bebop), new-age, country and countless fusions. Through the Gibson company the USA has also been responsible for the most fundamental rethink of mandolin design in the form of the carved instrument.

Overall, the mandolin's fortunes are rising and it is hoped that this book might aid the ascent. It is not my mission to preach any one kind of music or style of playing, rather to give a general introduction to the instrument in the hope that those inspired will go on to further musical exploration. In short, I have tried to be descriptive rather than prescriptive.

Ideally, the reader should use this book with a sympathetic teacher (the adjective is important). But as I lamented earlier, they are elusive creatures; and I have borne in mind that most people will of necessity be using it as a self-tutor.

Good luck!

CONTENTS

WHAT IS A MANDOLIN?

A rather well known radio DJ invited me in for interview one day. It would be the usual thing no doubt: play a couple of tunes, talk about the instrument, that sort of stuff. I arrived at the studio in good time and chatted to him before the programme. What sort of questions did he have in mind? "Oh, just general things..." he smiled, waving the air. We went into the studio. "A tune now from Simon Mayor" he announced. A quick musical burst followed and then he let me have it right between the eyes: "Tell me Simon, what is a mandolin?"

Believe it or not, it was the first time anyone had asked me this perfectly reasonable question. Just because I had been nutty about the instrument for years, just because I could tell you the serial number of Bill Monroe's Gibson F5, what gauge strings David Grisman used, why the thing is double strung, and what Vivaldi had for dinner on the day he wrote his mandolin concerto* didn't mean that the average listener should know what a mandolin was.

There was a pregnant pause as I gave a mental gasp at the stunningly simple relevance of the question, and mustered what I like to think was an adequate answer. The interview went smoothly after that, but I hope the incident had a beneficial effect on this book, in that I have tried to assume no prior knowledge of anything.

So, what is it?

A mandolin is a small, plucked, stringed instrument. Most cultures in the world have an instrument that fits this description, and the mandolin is the Italian variety. It is played on the knee like a guitar with a piece of plastic called a plectrum, but it is tuned like a violin. Whereas the violin has four strings, the mandolin has four *pairs* of strings, each pair tuned in unison (the reason for this will become clear before the end of the book). For all practical purposes, the mandolin can be thought of as having four strings.

The instrument you've got should look like one of the two main styles pictured opposite. Below is the traditional Italian round-back; above is the more modern American-designed flat-back. All round-backs are basically the same shape, but the level of decoration varies. Flat-backs vary more; some are teardrop shaped like the one pictured here, while others have decorative scrolls and points (like the Gibson carved mandolins mentioned earlier).

Take a few moments to learn the names of the parts.

---

* Four Seasons pizza with extra anchovies.

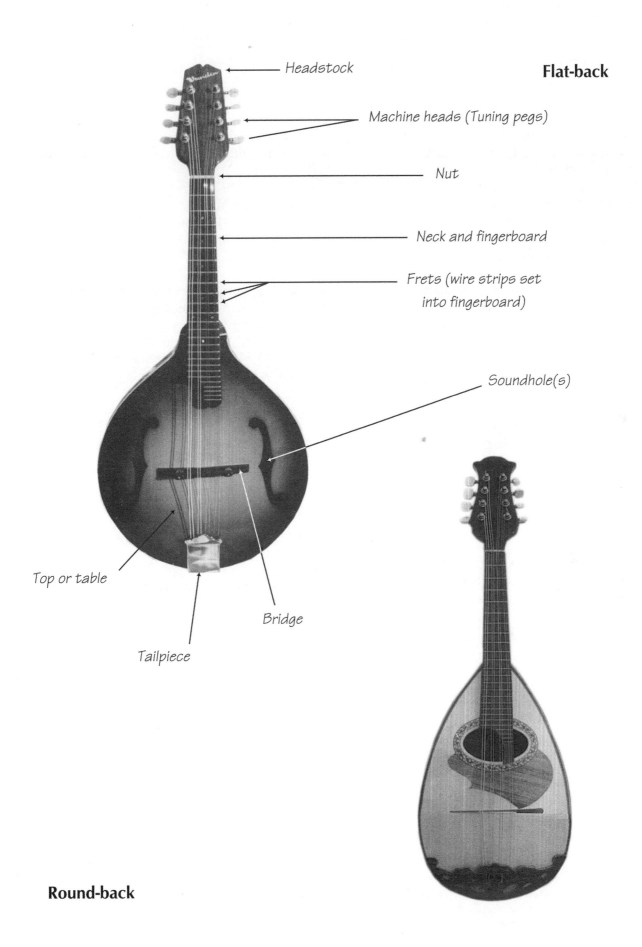

Headstock

Machine heads (Tuning pegs)

Nut

Neck and fingerboard

Frets (wire strips set
into fingerboard)

Soundhole(s)

Top or table

Tailpiece

Bridge

Flat-back

Round-back

FIRST THINGS FIRST

Are you sitting comfortably?

It's important to be comfortable to do anything well, and playing the mandolin is no exception.

CD ref. 3

Playing some musical instruments can make the player twist into awkward positions. Over the years the body might mould itself to an habitually distorted shape. Double bass players frequently develop backache, violinists get stiff necks and guitarists often have one shoulder higher than the other.

The mandolin is sufficiently small and manageable that horror stories like these needn't happen. Indeed they needn't with any instrument if you start as you mean to go on and avoid bad posture. You may be one of those people who naturally have a good posture, or you may need to be reminded of it. Many people have found Yoga or the Alexander Method a great help. These techniques are certainly worth investigating, but the common message is to be aware of any tensions in your body as you play and to do something about it before you do long term damage.

So with a bit of foresight and luck you shouldn't have problems, but a few thoughts might not go amiss....

◆ Don't practise for long periods. Little and often is much better for the body and the brain.

◆ Sitting cross-legged is generally not as comfortable as sitting with your legs apart, particularly for long periods. You may find a footstool helps.

◆ If you play a round-back, don't try standing up. Some professional players do stand to gain better projection in a concert hall, but the instrument really isn't designed for it. Although many flat-back players stand up to play, you'll find it easier to sit down when you're learning.

◆ If you do stand up, you *must* use a strap - but a word of warning. There is a trend among many bluegrass players to put the strap over just the right shoulder*. That shoulder is invariably hunched, and the whole body is put out of balance.

---

* This is something I never understood until a friend pointed out how difficult it is to get a strap over your head if you're wearing a Stetson hat. This is a vexing problem, but a brilliant solution has occurred to me: temporarily remove the Stetson to put the strap over your head! The Stetson should be replaced (as quickly as possible of course); this way you get the best of both worlds.

CD ref. 4 The mandolin is played with a plectrum or pick. The traditional material for this was tortoiseshell, but nowadays, quite rightly, plastic is used almost universally. You'll find a good selection in any music shop. I'd advise you start with one of medium size and thickness (about 0.7 to 0.8 mm). Try the shape outlined here: it's one of the most common and any music shop will be able to supply one. You'll want to experiment with shapes and thicknesses after you've learned the basics; I did, and boringly came back to a medium gauge pick which I've used for many years*.

CD ref. 5 Just as there is no right or wrong shape or thickness for a plectrum, there is no one 'correct' grip. Many experienced players use different grips, and I sometimes change grip during a tune for differing effects. This is food for future thought, but for now let's concentrate on the most commonly used method and the one which will probably feel most natural.

Curl the fingers of your right hand gently inwards and rest the plectrum across the last joint of the first finger as shown. Now grip it with the ball of your thumb. Think of the amount of pressure you use to hold a knife and fork; your plectrum grip should be similar - not too light, and not too firm.

Waggle it about a bit and get used to the feel. Try playing the open strings of the mandolin just with down strokes, getting used to the resistance of the strings as the notes sound. You may find you have to tighten your grip if the pick flies from your hand, or you may be able to relax a little if the resistance feels too great. There should be some 'give' as it crosses the string.

 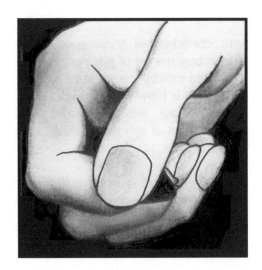

* To be accurate, the one pictured is the 5237th as I keep losing them.

TUNING

The machine heads are used to tune the strings. Tighten the string if it is too low in pitch, CD ref. 6 loosen it if it is too high. If you have the CD that goes with this book (strongly recommended of course), you can tune to the notes given.

Some people have a good idea of pitch right from the start. Others may find it difficult to hear whether or not a note is in tune. They may be able to tell that it is out of tune, but not be sure if it is *sharp* (too high) or *flat* (too low). Don't be too discouraged if you do have problems. If experienced help is not to hand you may wish to buy an **electronic tuner**. This is by far the easiest option; you needn't *hear* whether the strings are tune, you can *see* from the meter. Technology is wonderful, but it comes at quite a price.

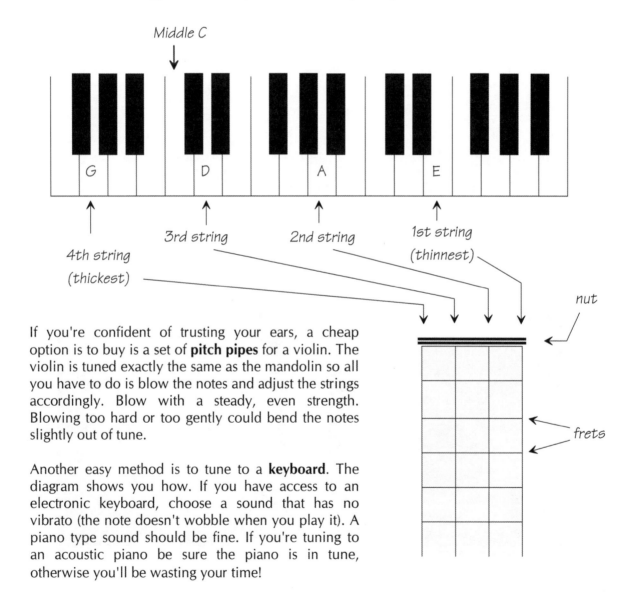

If you're confident of trusting your ears, a cheap option is to buy is a set of **pitch pipes** for a violin. The violin is tuned exactly the same as the mandolin so all you have to do is blow the notes and adjust the strings accordingly. Blow with a steady, even strength. Blowing too hard or too gently could bend the notes slightly out of tune.

Another easy method is to tune to a **keyboard**. The diagram shows you how. If you have access to an electronic keyboard, choose a sound that has no vibrato (the note doesn't wobble when you play it). A piano type sound should be fine. If you're tuning to an acoustic piano be sure the piano is in tune, otherwise you'll be wasting your time!

CD ref. 7

♦ Choose an A tuning fork and tune the second string to it (remember strings are numbered from the highest to the lowest so A is the second thinnest). Once the A is tuned, leave it alone!

♦ Now fret the D (third) string at the seventh fret. It should sound the same as the A string played open. If it doesn't, adjust it accordingly. Use the *tips* of your left hand fingers to press the strings - not directly on the metal frets, but onto the wood just behind them, otherwise the sound will be muffled (try it and hear).

♦ Next fret the A string at the seventh fret. It should sound the same as the E (first) string played open. If it doesn't, adjust the E string (not the A string).

♦ Finally fret the G (fourth) string at the seventh fret and tune it to the D string played open.

CD ref. 8

In theory, the mandolin will now be in tune, but any error between the second and third strings may have been magnified by the time you tuned the fourth string. If your ears are good try this cross check using octaves (for a fuller discussion of octaves see page 25).

♦ Fret the G string at the second fret. It should sound an octave below the A string played open.

♦ Similarly, the D string played on the second fret should sound an octave below the E string played open.

One last thing to mention: remember to tune up to pitch rather than down. Strings tend not to slip as easily if you do this.

READING TABLATURE

CD ref. 9

If you're coming to the mandolin from the guitar or violin (as many do) then there's a chance that you'll have learned the basics of reading music already. This, of course, will be a great help, but it isn't essential when you start.

To help those who don't read, this book uses the system of tablature in parallel with the music. Tablature, described below, is an ancient and beautifully simple way of notating music. You should be able to learn and use it very quickly.

Like standard music notation (and like the written word for that matter), tablature is a journey in time from left to right across the page. Although at first glance it looks similar to music, it works in a completely different way. The diagram should explain.

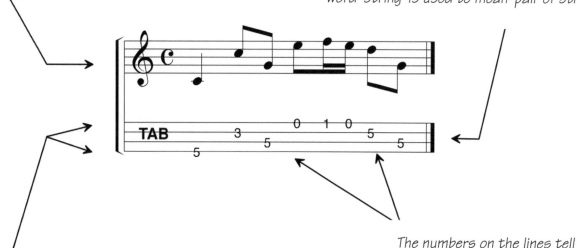

This top section is the standard music notation

This section is the tablature. The four horizontal lines represent the four strings of the mandolin (just to make things clear, I should point out that throughout this book the word 'string' is used to mean 'pair of strings')

The top line of the tablature staff is the E string (the thinnest and highest sounding), the bottom is the G (the thickest and lowest sounding)

The numbers on the lines tell you which fret to finger on that particular string. 'O' means play the open string. It really is that simple!

Yes, a plea! Use tablature as a means to get yourself kick-started, but don't become too seduced by its simplicity.

The problem with tablature is that it relates only to the mandolin; it is not a universal musical language. In other words, it is utterly meaningless to a trumpet player or a bamboo nose-flute virtuoso. Similarly, if by lesson six you decide you want to learn *The Flight Of The Bumblebee*, you are unlikely to find it published anywhere in mandolin tablature*, so as a long term goal you should aim to learn standard music notation as well. There's no doubt it is more complicated than tablature, but once it is mastered you will have the whole world at your disposal rather than one little island.

View this as a goal as you work your way through the book. You will, in any case, have to glance at the music to get the rhythm of the piece, as this is not expressed in the tablature. Since the music and tablature are always vertically aligned this shouldn't be a problem. I hope at least some of the tunes in the first few pages will be familiar to you. If not, a combination of the tablature and the CD should prove helpful. If you are unfamiliar with music notation and do not have the CD, you may like to flick forward to pages 28, 29, 36 and 38 where rhythm and note values are discussed.

Rather than bombard you with a long thesis on how to read music right at the start, 'Notation Stations' are staggered throughout the book. These sections will explain things gradually, and relate to whatever tune you're learning at the time.

If you want a complete crash course on reading music before you start to play, most music shops will be able to sell you one.

---

*   The author occasionally accepts special commissions.

THE OPEN STRINGS

Let's think first just about the open (unfretted) strings of the mandolin, these are the easiest of all notes to play. *CD ref. 10*

The notes, going up in pitch are called G, D, A and E. G is the thickest string (nearest your nose), E is the thinnest (nearest your toes).

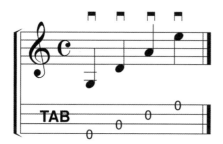

Don't worry about the left hand yet; just use it to cradle the neck of the mandolin. Be aware of the resistance of the strings as you cross them with the plectrum. Remember you need a medium grip; it should give a little as it strikes the strings. *CD ref. 11*

Play the strings with down strokes a few times as in the first example. The '0' on each line of the tablature staff simply indicates that each string should be played open.

The next example still works on the open strings, but use the plectrum alternately down and up. So in the second one it's down/up on the G string, then down/up on the D string etc.

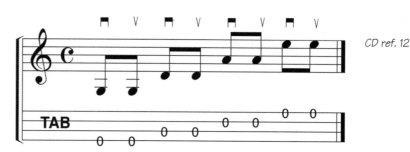

CD ref. 12

You'll find that it's easier to play the down strokes with more force. After all, you have gravity on your side. Nevertheless, as you play, listen to the sound you are making and try to play the up strokes with the same force as the downs to get a smooth even sound.

Notation Station

The small symbols above the notes are conventions used in violin music to indicate down strokes and up strokes. They'll suit us fine too, and may be of use to you if you use violin music at any point.

⊓   V

Down   Up

Examples 3 and 4 are a little more involved, but remember speed is not important, particularly in these early stages. Just try to keep the rhythm steady.

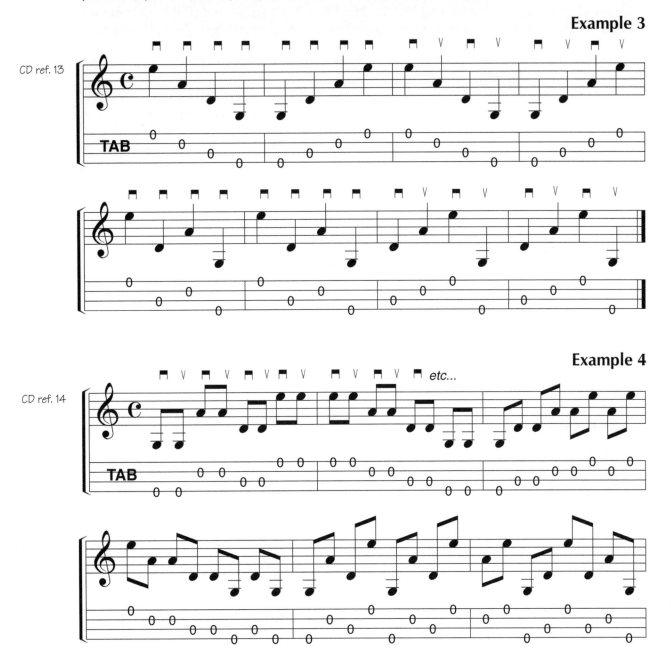

Example 3

CD ref. 13

Example 4

CD ref. 14

I've not indicated plectrum direction for every remaining note in every piece in the book, only where it may not be obvious or where I want you to try something in particular. You should experiment for yourself, but as a general rule, most people find a down-up-down-up pattern sounds most fluent most of the time. However, aim to start each bar with a down stroke; this will give it a natural emphasis.

THE LEFT HAND

When we play the open strings, they vibrate between the bridge and the nut. By pressing the *CD ref. 15* strings down with the left hand fingers we shorten the length of the string that vibrates when it is played. The shorter the vibrating length, the higher the note, so as you slide a finger up a string from the first fret towards the body you can hear the note rising. Try it.

Cradle the neck of the mandolin between your thumb and first finger. Don't let it fall fully into your hand, but support it gently between the first thumb joint and the side of the finger. The thumb will be protruding 2 or 3mm above the fingerboard and there should be a gap between the back of the neck and your hand big enough to waggle a pencil through.

Curl your fingers round in a fairly tight arch over the strings. Each joint should be bent (don't *CD ref. 16* let any collapse) with the final one falling near perpendicularly onto the fingerboard so that as you fret one string you don't catch the one next to it. You should find that your fingers are positioned not parallel to the frets, but angled half round towards the instrument's body, pointing roughly in the direction of your eyes. This is more akin to a violinist's hand position than a classical guitarist's, and something that most people find naturally comfortable on a mandolin. As I mentioned earlier, you should use the tips of your left hand fingers to press the strings onto the wood just behind the metal frets.

If it's really hard to press the strings down it could be that the action of the mandolin is too high (the *action* is the height of the strings above the fingerboard). Consult Appendix (ii); you may be able to take some steps yourself.

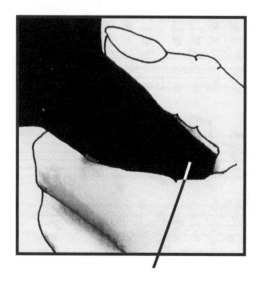

Leave a gap between the back of the neck and the hand.

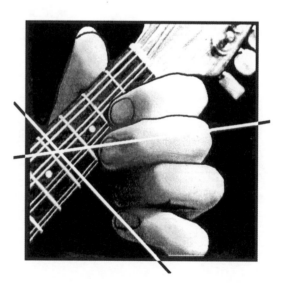

Fingering a G major chord (see page 32). The lines show how the fingers are not parallel to the frets.

CD ref. 17 We'll be concerned in this book with 'first position' fingerings, in other words notes found on the first seven frets of the mandolin. These frets can all be reached with the four left-hand fingers without moving the hand position. Unlike a guitar, where one finger generally covers one fret, the mandolin's scale length is shorter, so generally each finger covers two frets. The diagram shows the left hand:

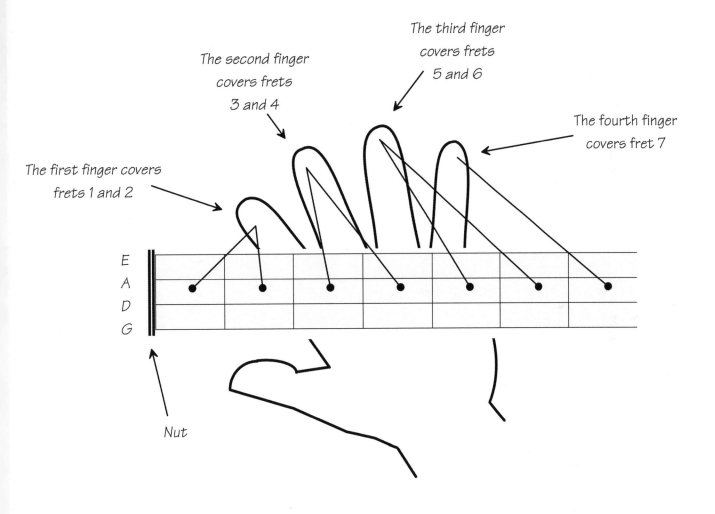

In practice, this is not as confusing as it might at first seem. Let's play the scale of A major (the top of the next page).

SCALING THE HEIGHTS

A *scale* just means a certain sequence of notes. The word *major* tells us in advance what the differing gaps are going to be between one note and the next. We needn't worry what those gaps are for the moment, but as you play the sequence will probably sound familiar and predictable. It is, after all, the basis of most Western music as immortalised by Julie Andrews singing "Doh, a deer, a female deer, ray, a drop of golden sun.....".

Scale of A major

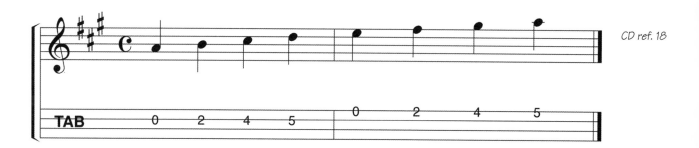

CD ref. 18

If you're following the tablature, remember the numbers on the lines (strings) tell you which *fret* you should be fingering.

Also, notice how the fingering pattern for the first string is the same as for the second string, and that you don't need to use your little finger at all here.

Here's exactly what should be happening...   *CD ref. 19*

- ◆ The second string is played open
- ◆ The first finger plays the second fret, second string
- ◆ The second finger plays the fourth fret, second string
- ◆ The third finger plays the fifth fret, second string
- ◆ The first string is played open
- ◆ The first finger plays the second fret, first string
- ◆ The second finger plays the fourth fret, first string
- ◆ The third finger plays the fifth fret, first string

The second example is the scale of D major. You'll notice that the pattern of fingering is exactly the same as for an A major scale. All that has happened is that the whole pattern has been shifted one string lower. Instead of starting on the open second string, this scale starts on the third. The last example shifts the same pattern onto the bottom two strings to give us a G major scale.

Scale of D major

CD ref. 20

Scale of G major

CD ref. 21

Notation Station

Try to memorise these scales: they're just a simple recurring pattern and you shouldn't find it too difficult.

As you play them, look at the music even though you may not understand it. Notice how the notes rise *visually* as they rise in pitch.

A DOSE OF DIGITAL DEXTERITY

Now it's time to get your left hand fingers moving and to have some fun with the scales: CD ref. 22 play up, play down, play all with down strokes, then play with alternate down and up strokes. Here are a couple of exercises. They're patterns that repeat as you move up and down the scale, and should feel predictable once you've played them a few times.

Dose 1

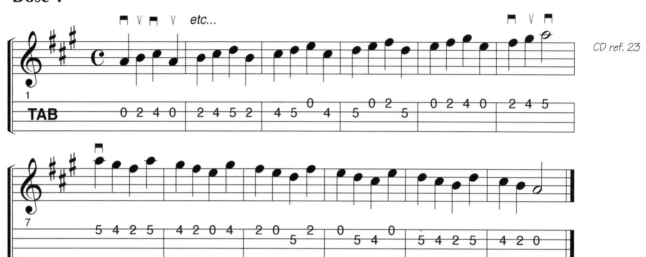

CD ref. 23

Dose 2

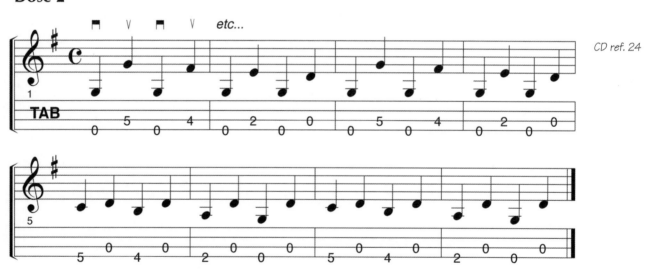

CD ref. 24

It's important to think about economy of movement. Keep your fingers close to the fingerboard all the time, even when they are not fretting a note. If you wave them up in the air you'll only have to bring them down onto the fingerboard again.

Now it's time to play some tunes using the notes in one of these scales. The great composers weren't averse to using scales as part of a tune so we might as well start at the top. Here's a (slightly simplified) version of one of Beethoven's best known pieces, using the scale of A major.

Ode To Joy

Notice how there are few jumps in the melody; for most of the tune the notes just move either up or down to the next one in the scale.

Notation Station

The horizontal bracket linking the last note of bar 12 to the first of bar 13 is called a *tie*. It means that the first note of bar 13 is not played, but the previous note is lengthened to compensate. We'll discuss note values in more detail on page 28 but if you have the CD, you should hear the effect easily enough.

The Floral Dance

The Floral Dance is a traditional tune from the West Country. It has quite a few versions, some very popular with brass bands, but this one is used for country dancing. It's written here using the scale of A major. Use down strokes apart from the quavers (the notes with linked stems) where you should alternate down and up.

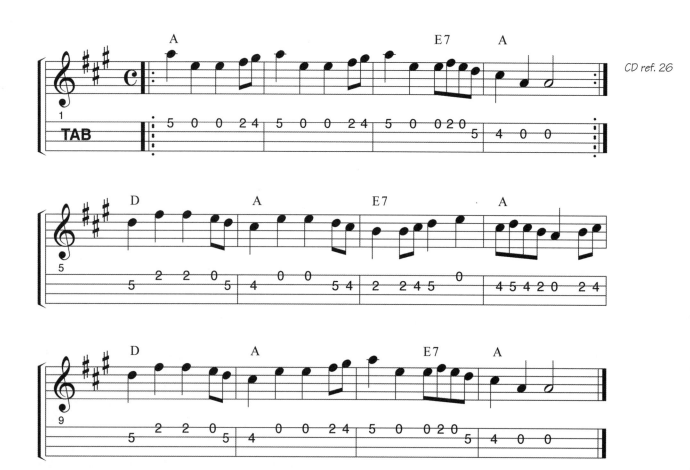

CD ref. 26

When you've played this tune a few times, see if you can memorise it; it's just as important to develop this skill as it is to read music.

If you can, try and play it using the scale of D major. The entire fingering pattern transfers one string lower so the first note would be a D found on the second string, fifth fret.

Transfer the entire pattern two strings lower and you'll be playing it in G major.

Here's another simple tune, this time from America. Some sections of it simply move up and down the steps of the scale (D major this time), but, as with *The Floral Dance*, there are jumps as well.

CD ref. 27

Notation Station

Any passage of music that should be repeated is enclosed by these special bar lines:

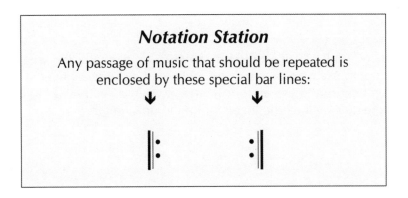

HEIGHTENING THE SCALES (G)

There's no getting away from it: scales are deadly boring to play for their own sake, but they do serve a purpose. They are the framework within which a tune is written. If we know scales, we will always have a reasonable idea of what shape a tune is going to take. Our fingers will be ready to play the right fret because we know that the notes of a tune are all taken from a particular sequence.

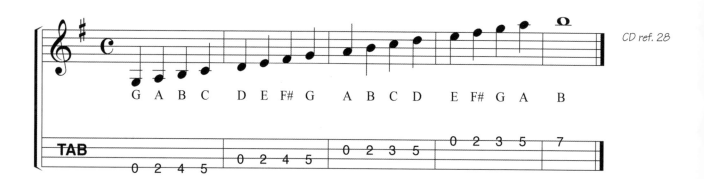

CD ref. 28

The scales we learned earlier were just one octave segments, only part of the whole picture. Here's the scale of G again, but this time going two octaves and two notes up from the bottom G string. The names of the notes are printed below so you can see how the sequence repeats.

The highest note of *Wildwood Flower* went to the top string, outside the scale of D major that we practised on page 19. So scales don't stop with the octave (eight notes) we learned; the sequence just repeats up or down as far as the instrument will allow.

Make your pinky perky

The last note of B in the scale above is the first time you've had to use your little finger. It's not easy, is it?

CD ref. 29

The fourth finger, or 'pinky' as it's called in America, is naturally the weakest. Because of this it's tempting not to use it and jump to the note with a stronger finger. Take my word for it: it's easier in the long run to use all four fingers, so start as you mean to go on. The more you use it, the more quickly the little finger will build up strength.

CD ref. 30   The notes in music take their names from the first seven letters of the alphabet. When the eighth, or *octave* is reached, the names start again.

You might wonder why we don't use all twenty six letters as names. The reason for this is that an octave is a very important pitch gap in music. Have a look at these three notes, all called G.

Without getting too deeply into the science of acoustics, you'll notice as you play them that, although they are far apart in pitch, they sound essentially the same.

You can play all three notes together and, provided your instrument is in tune, they will sound more like one note with a very rich resonance. First play the three notes separately and then strum quickly across all three. Incidentally, you'll have to use your first and fourth fingers of your left hand to get these notes.

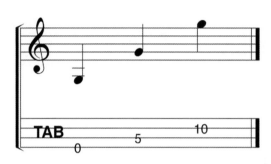

So any note can be found at various places on the fingerboard in different octaves. Here are two more examples, D and A respectively.

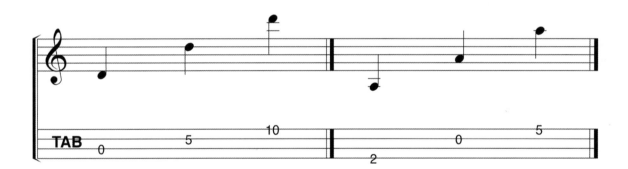

Notation Station

On some tunes, you may have noticed symbols above the music (G, Am, D7, etc). These are chord symbols used so that accompanists (guitarists or pianists) can improvise a part. A chord simply means a collection of notes played at once. They can be strummed on a guitar or 'vamped' on a piano and are used to support the melody. You can play chords on a mandolin too, and we'll be looking at them soon.

TUNES IN TWO OCTAVES OF G

Now here are two more tunes to demonstrate what I was just saying about octaves. Each tune is written first in the lower octave of the G scale and then in the upper octave.

Buffalo Girls

CD ref. 31

On Ilkley Moor Bah T'at

The guitar chords remain the same for the lower and upper octave of each tune, indeed the tune remains the same, the only difference is that the second time round is higher. Incidentally, you have to use your little finger in this one so beware!

CD ref. 32

MAINLINE NOTATION STATION

CD ref. 33

With a bit of luck, you will have known at least some of the tunes we've already played, so you should have been able to hear if you were getting things right. Before long, we'll be looking at tunes you won't be familiar with, so these will be your first exercises in reading. If you're doubtful about the conventional notation you can always read the tablature to find which note you should be on. However, the rhythm of the piece is not shown in the tablature, so you will have to look at the music for that. Remember the two are always vertically aligned, so this shouldn't be a problem. The *rhythm* simply means how long each note lasts. Here's a simple guide.

CD ref. 34

- ◆ All notes have a head which is either open (**o**) or black (**●**)

- ◆ An open note with no stem is called a *semibreve* and is four beats long (**o**)

- ◆ An open note with a stem is called a *minim* and is two beats long (𝅗𝅥)

- ◆ A black note with a stem is called a *crotchet* and is one beat long (♩)

- ◆ A black note with a stem and tail is a *quaver* and is half a beat long (♪)

- ◆ If two or more quavers come next to each other they are often joined instead of having tails (♫)

It doesn't matter at all whether stems go up or down;
the value of the note is not affected.

So one semibreve   **o**

lasts as long as two minims   𝅗𝅥   𝅗𝅥

or four crotchets   ♩   ♩   ♩   ♩

or eight quavers   ♪ ♪ ♪ ♪ ♪ ♪ ♪ ♪

Lets consider one brief example. Sing the first line of *Baa Baa Black Sheep* to yourself and tap your foot at the same time. The crosses show where your foot should tap:

Baa	baa,	black	sheep,	have you	an - y	wool?	
✗	✗	✗	✗	✗	✗	✗	

The first four syllables are all one beat long. In other words they each have one foot-tap on them. The two syllables 'have' and 'you' are half beats, squashed into one foot-tap. So are 'an - ' and 'y'. The syllable 'wool' is two beats long. So here's what the rhythm looks like in musical notation:

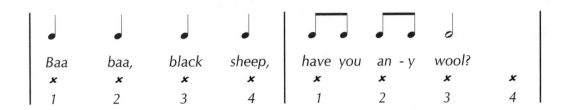

It doesn't matter too much if you don't remember the names of the note values, but get used to recognising their lengths. To help you along I've put the count underneath.

If you want an extra little exercise, you could try working out the melody of this tune, say in the key of D major. It would start on the note of D (third string played open). Memorise it if you can, then try jotting it down in either music or tablature.

HEIGHTENING THE SCALES (D)

Back to some tunes, but first let's look at a more extensive version of the D major scale, going both above and below the octave segment we learned earlier. The lowest note of D to be found on the mandolin is the third string played open, so to go below this we start part way up the scale on the G (bottom string). You have to play the G string at the sixth fret; use your third finger for this.

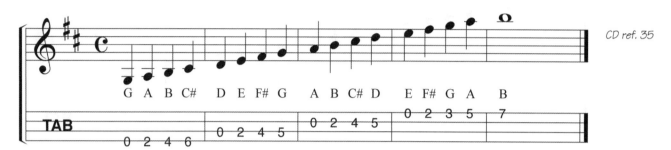

CD ref. 35

In case you hadn't realised, a scale takes its name from its first note, or *root* note. If a tune is constructed using notes from a D major scale, we say it is in the *key* of D major. You'll find that it's very common for a tune in a particular key to finish on the root note; somehow it feels the most natural place to end, and the tune feels complete.

CD ref. 36

This is true of the next two tunes. I'm not going to tell you the titles but they're both Christmas favourites. You should recognise them with no problem.

Christmas tune 1

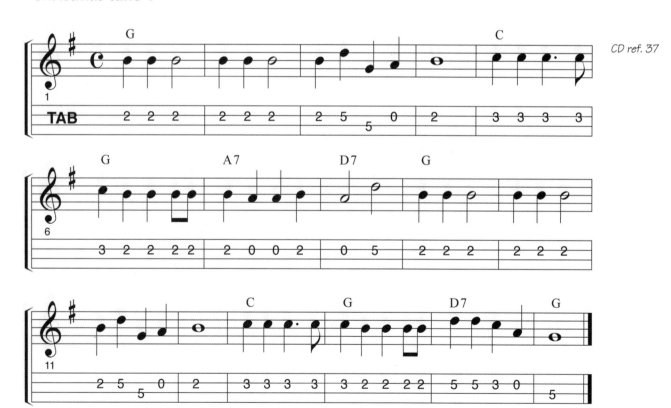

CD ref. 37

CHORDS

I gave a brief mention to chords on page 25. Chord symbols can be used by mandolinists as well; the mandolin is not widely thought of as an accompanying instrument, but it can be really effective in this role.

To start with, we'll look at some of the easier open chords. By *open*, I mean chords that use one or more of the open strings.

You may have heard musicians talk of the 'three chord trick'. There are hundreds and hundreds of simple songs and tunes that can be accompanied by just three chords, and these are based on the first (root), fourth and fifth notes of the particular scale being used. The first and fourth chords are usually played as majors; the fifth can be played as a 7th.

CD ref. 39

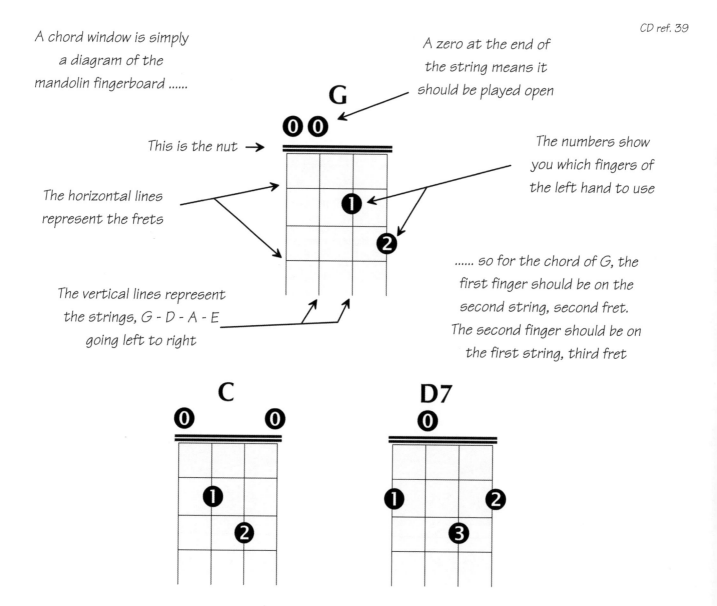

A chord window is simply a diagram of the mandolin fingerboard ......

A zero at the end of the string means it should be played open

G

This is the nut →

The numbers show you which fingers of the left hand to use

The horizontal lines represent the frets

...... so for the chord of G, the first finger should be on the second string, second fret. The second finger should be on the first string, third fret

The vertical lines represent the strings, G - D - A - E going left to right

C

D7

CD ref. 40 When a chord is named simply by a letter (G, C, D, etc.) we assume it is a *major* chord; in other words the notes in it come from a major scale. Some chords have suffixes in their name (for example Em, G7); these tell us something else about the nature of the sound we are going to hear.

The suffix 'm' means the notes in it are taken from a minor scale. We haven't learned a minor scale yet but it doesn't matter. When you play a minor chord you should hear that it sounds different - more melancholy in character - from a major chord. Try changing between G and Gm and you should hear what I mean. You can flick forward to pages 38 and 39 for discussion of minors keys.

A chord with the suffix '7' is similar to a major, but has an extra note taken from outside the major scale. It sounds somehow incomplete and leads naturally back to the root major chord.

Now go back to page 22 and have another look at *The Floral Dance*. The chords used are A (first or root), D (fourth) and E7 (fifth). If you have the CD that goes with this book, swing the balance control on your stereo hard left so you just hear the melody and play along strumming the chords.

Here and overleaf is a dictionary of the more common chords used on the mandolin. Notice similarities; you will find patterns re-occur in chords just as they do in scales. For example, a C chord is the same basic shape as G, but one string lower (make sure the top string rings clear). Only the second string differs a G from a Gm. Similarly, Gm is the same shape as Bm four frets nearer to the nut.

CD ref. 41
CD ref. 42

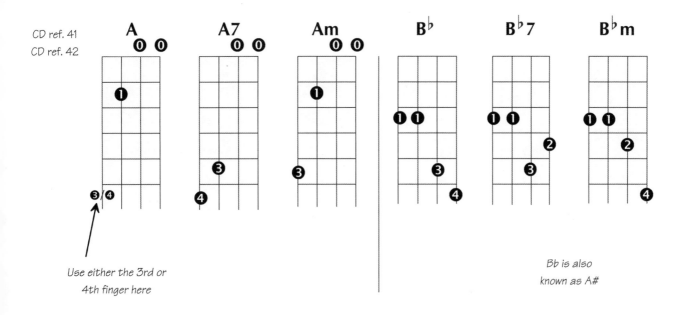

Use either the 3rd or
4th finger here

Bb is also
known as A#

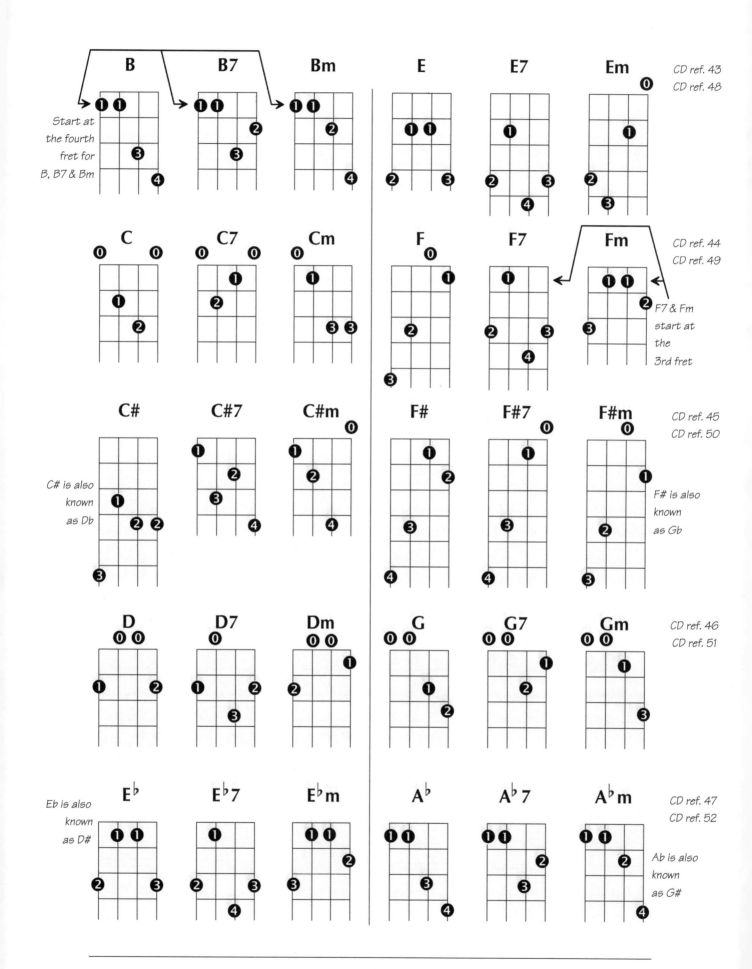

CD ref. 53 There are many chords here that you will not need at all in this book, and many which will seem impossible to finger at the moment. All the same, they will come in handy for reference.

There are occasions when you need to cover more than one string with one finger (usually the first); this is known as a *barre* and involves pressing the strings down with the ball instead of the tip of the finger.

Practise strumming lightly across all the strings aiming for a smooth sound with as little plectrum noise as possible. Don't rest your right hand on the instrument at all, but raise it a few millimetres above and use a swift but light flick of the right wrist. You'll find the tone will vary between a harsh metallic sound if you play near the bridge and a more mellow sound over the end of the fingerboard. The same is true when you play tunes, of course.

HEIGHTENING THE SCALES (A)

Picking up where we left off on page 30, you should have recognised *Good King Wenceslas* and *Jingle Bells*. While we're in a Christmas mood we'll try another carol, *O Come All Ye Faithful*, this time in the key of A major. First let's play a more extensive A major scale starting on the seventh note (G#) found on the first fret of the bottom string. The first finger is used for this and the following A.

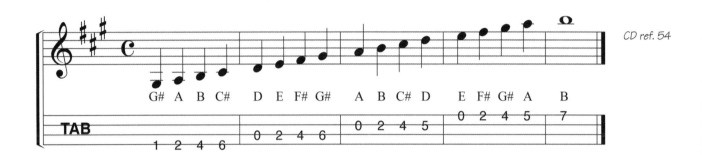

CD ref. 54

Within first position, we can get up to a top B (use your fourth finger), which is just one note into the third octave of the scale.

CD ref. 55

Notation Station

"He ain't got rhythm so no-one's with 'im, the loneliest man in town"

As you play the next tune, think some more about rhythm.

You'll notice in bars 8, 13 and 20 these two notes:

If a note is followed by a dot it increases its length by half.

So a dotted crotchet   is 1½ beats long.

If a pair of crotchets   (1 + 1 = 2)

are replaced by a dotted crotchet and a quaver   (1½ + ½ = 2)

we still end up with notes to the value of two beats, but the dotted rhythm will inject a little skip into it. Don't think about this too hard, just play the tune *as you know it* and you should hear what I mean.

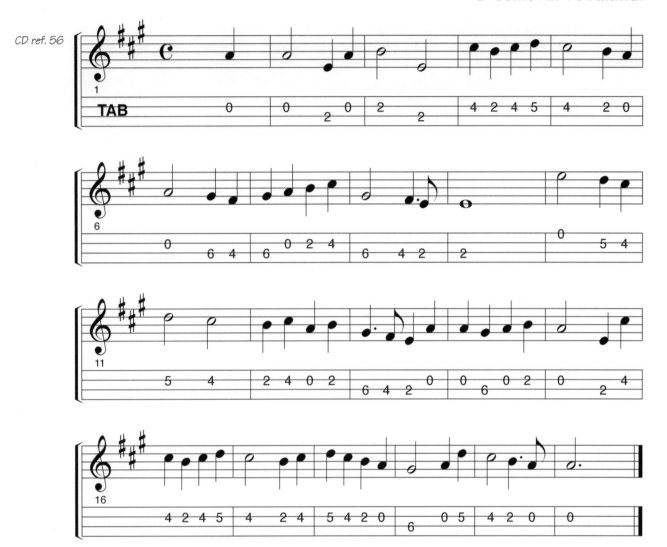

You may find in the third bar of the tune (over the word 'faithful' if you sing along) that it is difficult to make the notes sound steady and even. This is because you have to move very quickly with your left hand first finger from the notes B to E, that is from the syllables 'faith' to 'ful'.

There are a couple of ways you can get round this problem. The most common is to fret both strings at once with the ball instead of the tip of your first finger. That way, the first note rings on a little while you are playing the second and doesn't sound so chopped off.

The other way is to fret the B (first note of the third bar) with the second instead of the first finger, then tuck your first finger behind it to get the following note of E. If you have marrow* fingers this may appeal more. From then on you can go back to using the tips of your fingers.

---

*   This was a typing error. It should read 'narrow fingers'.

¾ TIME

CD ref. 57

I hope you've had an instinctive feel for the rhythm of the tunes we've learned so far - where the pulse comes. They've all had four beats to the bar, but music would be boring if this were always the case.

The other most frequently encountered time signature in Western music is ¾ time, often called waltz time, which has three beats to the bar. Instead of 1 - 2 - 3 - 4, 1 - 2 - 3 - 4, we count 1 - 2 - 3, 1 - 2 - 3 etc. *The Star of the County Down* is in ¾ time.

CD ref. 58

Notation Station

Bar lines

Bar lines (the vertical black lines) divide the music up into equal numbers of beats - it could be three, four or whatever. All the tunes we've learned so far have had four beats, so each bar could be made up from, for example -

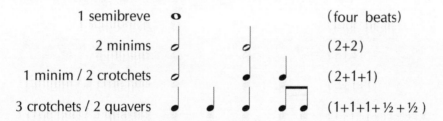

1 semibreve	(four beats)
2 minims	(2+2)
1 minim / 2 crotchets	(2+1+1)
3 crotchets / 2 quavers	(1+1+1+ ½ + ½)

- or various other permutations. Take any bar and the total value of the notes will always be four beats.

Bar lines are very important because they tell us where the pulse comes in the music. The beat with most emphasis is the first beat of the bar. Still with *O Come All Ye Faithful* in mind this falls on the syllables 'come', 'faith', 'joy' and (appropriately) 'umph' etc.

Minor Keys

CD ref. 59

Although *The Star of the County Down* uses the scale of D, it is not in the key of D. Just as we were noticing the difference between major and minor chords, major and minor keys have a different flavour from each other. Each major key has a relative minor; this minor key uses the same notes of the scale but starts on the sixth note. In other words, this sixth note turns into the root note of the relative minor, and gives its name to that key. So the relative minor of D major is B minor, and *The Star of the County Down* is in this key. Unlike major scales, minors do have a few variations on the theme. This particular one, which simply starts on the sixth note of its relative major scale, is usually referred to as a natural minor scale.

It may be a huge generalisation, but tunes in a major key tend to have a happy, positive feel (e.g. *New York New York, The National Anthem, Ob-la-di Ob-la-da*) whereas tunes in a minor key have a more melancholy feel (e.g. *Eleanor Rigby, The Sound Of Silence, Greensleeves*).

JUST DEUX IT

Music was made for sharing*, both with an audience and other musicians, and I can't stress too strongly how important it is to play with other people. Even if you can't find a mandolin teacher, try and beg half an hour of a friend's time to play along with you. It doesn't matter if that friend isn't a mandolinist; the encouragement you'll gain from some simple accompaniment will be enormous.

Unless you're particularly into old English dances, the next three tunes may not be so familiar. If you're learning by yourself, just try the parts for the first mandolin; if you have a musical partner you can try them as duets. The melody and harmony lines are just as easy (or difficult) as each other, so you can try both.

Shepherd's Hey

CD ref. 61

---

*   the author's lapses into philosophy can be embarrassing.

The Phœnix looks simple, but there are a few things to watch. In bar 4 of the 1st mandolin part the high B should be played with the fourth finger. In bar 3 play the first note (D) by rocking the third finger back from the previous G. Try and give the tune a sense of fluency and sustain by allowing the G to ring for a split second underneath the D (hear on the CD).

Similar problems occur in the 2nd mandolin part, but a different solution is preferable. The high Ds in bars 3 and 4 should be played with the fourth finger; that way the preceeding Gs can ring on better. Use the fourth finger also for the Gs on the last note of bar 7 and the second of bar 8 so the third finger is free to fret the intervening C. All this is certainly easier if you have slim fingers, but accuracy is the most inportant thing.

The Phœnix

CD ref. 62

THE KEY OF F

Before we play the next tune, lets learn the key of F; it shouldn't pose too many problems. Although the high B♭ is on the sixth fret, it makes sense to use your fourth finger.

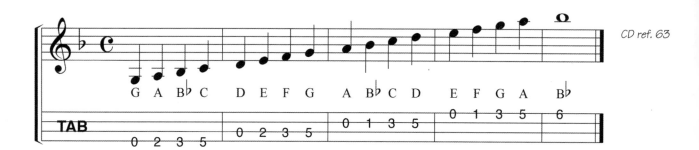

CD ref. 63

The next tune, *Nonesuch*, is the third old English dance, again arranged as a duet. The second mandolin part has an interesting piece of left hand fingering in bars 2 and 3. Finger the E in bar 2 with the second finger, the next note (B♭) with the first finger, then the open A string, and from then on in normal first position fingerings. The reason for doing this is to avoid an awkward jump with the first finger from the E to the B♭. This occurs again in bars 6 and 7.

The very last note of the second mandolin part involves striking the open D and A strings together. Try not to hit the G or E strings as you do this.

Nonesuch

CD ref. 64

Bourrée

Bourrée is another duet; a favourite from Handel's *Water Music*. It is possible to play both parts with standard first position fingering, but in some bars (of the standard music notation) I've indicated alternatives for the left hand which will aid fluency.

CD ref. 65

AFTER THE TRILL IS GONE

CD ref. 66

Tremolo is a bit of a cheat really! It's a way of giving the impression of a long sustained note by actually playing lots of short ones in rapid succession. Mandolinists, however, are skilled at making virtue out of necessity, and tremolo has became the sound the instrument is famous for, used in countless corny Hollywood B-movies by some actorrrrrr on bended knee beneath an open window serenading the object of his heart's desire! Love it or hate it, tremolo is an important weapon in the mandolinist's armoury.

You may have been wondering since page 6 why the mandolin is double strung. When we play tremolos on a double strung instrument we get twice as many notes for every stroke of the plectrum, and so a smoother tremolo. Simple!

Some people are blessed with an instinctive ability to turn on the trill. Others have to learn. You should aim to develop a controlled tremolo, not a wild flurry of fast notes, and the way to do it is to subdivide. Try the first example below on the open E string - the note values halve in each successive bar. In other words, with each bar you have to cram twice as many notes into the same amount of time.

If you have a metronome or a drum machine use it set to about $\quad$ = **50** at first, which is very slow, then increase the speed as you get used to it.

There are some adjustments you will need to make to your right hand technique. There is a notion that a loose wrist is all you need for a good tremolo; this is a popular misconception. Your wrist should indeed remain loose, but a good tremolo originates from the elbow. It is virtually impossible to play the demisemiquavers in the last bar of the example at any speed without some movement coming from the elbow. If you don't believe me, strap your arm to your body and see how you get on. Better still, try and watch somebody else doing it. It's a long shot, but if you ever get the chance try to see a visiting Russian folk group. Russian 'folk' musicians are invariably the product of many years intense training in music colleges and have quite astonishing technical ability. Tremolo is such an integral part of the balalaika and domra repertoire that this would be as worthwhile as seeing a good mandolinist.

Tremolo example 1

CD ref. 67

CD ref. 68

You've probably worked out for yourself that you can't rest your wrist on the strings behind the bridge for tremolo. Your arm should hover over the strings, but a millimetre or two above is all that is necessary. In time, this will become second nature as you burst into your impersonation of a hummingbird.

Overleaf are a couple of simple tunes to play tremolo. Don't, whatever you do, try to go too fast. While ultimately your tremolo should sound like a smoothly running, perfectly tuned little engine, it really doesn't matter at this early stage if it sounds like the individual notes that it is. The important thing is to keep it steady.

Notation Station

There's a bit of musical shorthand used here, and in the tunes overleaf.

A triple slash across a note means it should be played tremolo.

We use this if just selected notes from a piece are to be tremmed. If the whole piece is to be played tremolo an instruction is usually given at the start.

Lullaby Waltz

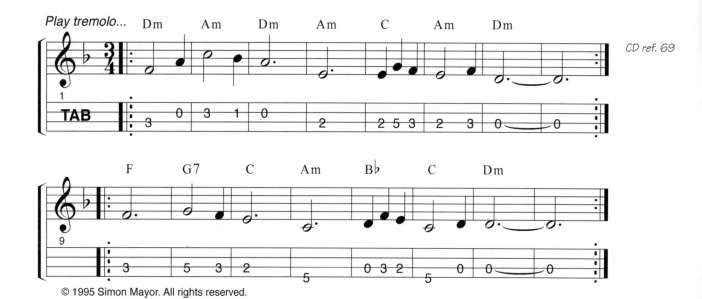

This is not a difficult tune, but try to keep the tremolo steady throughout. There will inevitably be a split second break in the tremolo when you have to cross strings, but this will sound smoother with practice.

A plea

It is the unfortunate lot of those in the early stages of learning to have to suffer instruments that can better be described as mandolin shaped boxes than mandolins. These plywood monstrosities usually have so little natural sustain that their owners, mastering the art of tremolo, are tempted to over-use it to compensate.

Now hear a plea for self-restraint and for good taste!

Tremolo, if over-used, can sound syrupy and ultimately very tiring on the ear. Use it sparingly and it will be twice as effective! Use it where it is least expected and it will take the listener completely by surprise and make the heart soar! One day you will treat yourself to a good mandolin. You'll put your head down to get closer to the sound and you'll play for two whole days without pause for eating or sleeping or other useless pursuits. You'll marvel at the craftspersonship, the ease of playing, and the greater natural sustain.

But for now let's play another tune with tremolo. This time don't use it on every note, just the ones marked with triple slashes.

MAINLINE NOTATION STATION

The pitch of a note (how high or low it is) is indicated by where its head sits on the staff; this can be either on a line or in a space. Any notes too high or low to fit on the staff have tiny extension lines called ledger lines. Unlike tablature, music usually looks like it sounds: if a note is higher up the staff, it will sound higher. Opposite you can see the names of the notes on the staff and where they are found on the mandolin. If you play them upwards, you will be playing up the scale of C major. It's the exact equivalent of playing up the white notes on a piano.

CD ref. 71

There are memory aids to help us remember where the notes fall on the staff. Going up, the spaces spell the word **FACE**. The favourite way of remembering the notes on the lines always used to be the sentence *Every Good Boy Deserves Favour,* but I prefer a different one...

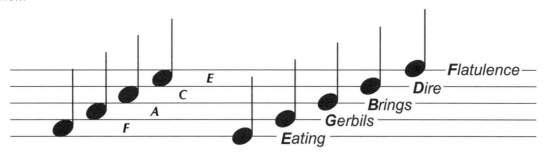

So where are the 'black' notes on the mandolin? Well, you've already been using them in many of the tunes you've already played. In the key of G major, for example, every note of F is played sharp. This means it is raised in pitch to the half-note or *semitone* above; this would be the black note above F on a piano, but on a mandolin it is the next fret above an F. So instead of the third fret, third string we play the fourth fret, and instead of the first fret top string we play the second fret.

CD ref. 72

We use the symbol ♯ at the beginning of every staff to show this. In the key of G major it appears on the note of F (the top line), but it implies that all Fs in whatever octave are played sharp. Have a glance back through some of the tunes in G that you've already played and you'll notice this. This is called the *key signature.* Each key has a a different number of sharps or flats. Here's a summary of the ones we meet in this book.

♦ In the key of C major (or A minor) there are no sharps or flats.

♦ In the key of G major (or E minor), all Fs are played sharp.

♦ In the key of D major (or B minor), all Fs and Cs are played sharp.

♦ In the key of A major (or F# minor), all Fs, Cs and Gs are played sharp.

♦ In the key of F major (or D minor), all Bs are played flat, one fret lower as shown by

   the ♭ symbol.

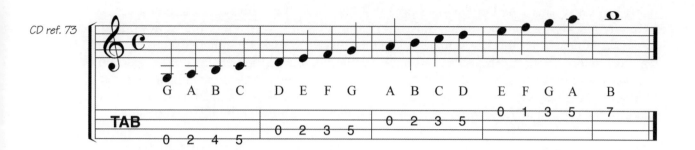

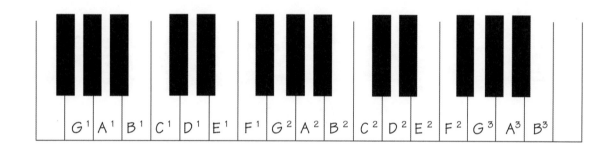

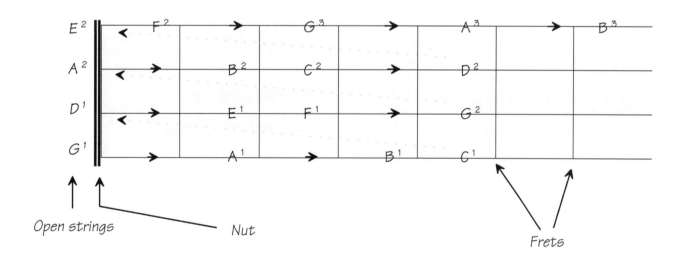

The diagrams show how the scale of C major corresponds to the white notes on a piano and where the same notes are found on the mandolin fingerboard.

ACCIDENTALS

CD ref. 74

No, these final pages have nothing to do with hospitals or dentistry! An accidental is the name given to a sharpened or flattened note that (get this....!) has been put there *on purpose* by the composer to give the tune a different colour. In other words, the tune strays outside the scale indicated by the key signature. Accidentals are shown by either a sharp or a flat sign just before the note. This affects all notes of that pitch until the next bar line is reached; the bar line effectively cancels the accidental. If the composer wants to cancel an accidental before the next bar, she uses this sign, ♮ called a natural. A natural is also used to cancel a sharp or flat present in the key signature; once again this is cancelled by the next barline.

Accidentals are common in all sorts of music. Here are two tunes that incorporate them.

Sharp As Nails

CD ref. 75

Mudflat Blues is a basic 12-bar blues. The blues was meant to be played rather than written down, so it looks more difficult than it really is, but if you have the CD you should pick it up fairly easily. Standard first position fingering is abandoned in a few places, so follow the recommendations for the left hand in the music.

HOW DO I CHOOSE A MANDOLIN?

There are two main sorts of mandolin: round-backs (Neapolitan style) and flat-backs. They do sound different, although (if we're honest with ourselves) only to mandolinists. Play a recording of either to the man-in-the-street and he may recognise it as a mandolin but won't have a clue as to which sort. I know, I know, the stupidity of the general public can be breathtaking! Anyway, let's get one thing straight from the start: it really doesn't matter which you play. Round-backs tend to be favoured by most classical players; their tone is bright and piercing. Flat-backs are used by those into folk, bluegrass and jazz; their's is a thicker, more rounded tone with more of a 'bloom' round the note. This doesn't mean you can't play folk on a roundback (many do) or classical on a flatback (I do).

So, the last thing I would want to do is to influence which sort of mandolin you ultimately settle with. It depends what sort of sound you like and what your primary musical interests are. However, certain facts (as opposed to prejudices) may affect your choice of instrument to start on.

First, flat-backs are without question easier to hold, particularly if you've got a beer gut. If you do buy a round-back you may want to drape a chammy leather over the back to stop it wobbling on your belly.

Second, beware the beautiful old Italian round-back covered with acres of mother-of-pearl. It lurks in corners of junk shops or in small ads in local newspapers waiting for gullible would-be-mandolinists to fork out hard earned cash. Its neck is bent, its top is sunk and the cost of repair is usually more than the instrument is worth. Pay £1 for it, hang it on the wall as an ornament and it will be money well spent. If you want a round-back to use as a musical instrument, go to a music shop and buy one with a straight neck, a playable action and a guarantee!

Thousands of Italian made round-backs were produced for the tourist trade around the turn of the century and were poorly built. The problem is the neck to body joint which is inherently weaker in the round-back design. Necessity being the mother of invention, the Americans designed the sturdier flat-back as all their imported round-backs fell apart in the variable climate.

Hand made instruments of either ilk, where much greater care has gone into the construction, will normally give no bother (and a better sound), but of course a price has to be paid for this.

Buying second-hand can sometimes be a good idea provided you know what you're looking for. If you're at all unsure take someone along who knows more than you do. This needn't be a mandolinist; any experienced guitarist will know what to look out for in buying a second hand guitar, and the principles are exactly the same for mandolins....

♦ Make sure the neck is straight, because if it isn't a repair will probably be expensive and may even cost more than the instrument is worth. Hold the mandolin as if you're firing a rifle and sight down the neck from the tailpiece. Any warping should be evident.

♦ Another method is to press a string down simultaneously on the first and last fret. There should be just enough room to slide a piece of paper between the strings and frets at about the 9th fret. Any larger gap means that the neck has probably bent forwards. If the string goes flat against all the frets when you try this test, the neck may have bent backwards, although this is uncommon as the pull of the strings is in the opposite direction.

♦ Check the mandolin carefully for any cracks or loose trim. Check that the sides are not pulling away from the back or top.

♦ Damp the strings with your hands and gently tap all over the body, listening for rattles and buzzes. If you hear any, it may mean that one of the braces inside has come loose. Braces are thin strips of wood glued to the inside of the mandolin; you can usually feel them through the soundhole. They are not there just for structural stability, but affect the tone quality of the instrument as well (the bracing patterns differ for roundbacks, flat-backs with F-holes and flat-backs with round holes). Once again, repair would be expensive, so if you suspect anything is wrong don't buy.

♦ Turn the machine heads. They should feel smooth and positive with no tight or loose spots.

♦ What's your general impression? Does the mandolin look as if it's been cared for? Old instruments inevitably pick up some scratches, but it's usually fairly obvious if the thing has been abused.

♦ Finally, make sure you know the market value of what you're buying.

TROUBLESHOOTING

It's so discouraging trying to learn on an instrument that is not in good playing condition. There may be some steps you can take yourself to improve matters.

The mandolin is difficult to tune

The most usual cause of this is the position of the bridge. Most guitars have a *fixed* bridge, one that is glued to the top of the guitar. Mandolins have a *floating* bridge, one that is held in place solely by the tension of the strings. If the bridge is wrongly positioned, even by half a millimetre, the mandolin will play out of tune. Here's how to check.

Rest the tip of a left hand finger on the E string directly over the 12th fret (the metal not the wood); do not press down. A fraction of a second after you pluck the string, lift the finger off. You should hear a bell like sound called a harmonic. It may take a little practise to get this but persevere, your new found technique will one day be put to more musical effect! The harmonic will sound exactly an octave above the open string. Now fret the E string at the 12th fret and play it. The sound should be the same pitch as the harmonic even though it is a different timbre. Make a note of any discrepancy and repeat the proceedure for the other three strings.

If the harmonics are lower in pitch than the fretted notes, the bridge should be moved towards the tailpiece. If the fretted notes are lower than the harmonics, the bridge should be moved towards the fingerboard. The movement needed might even be less than a millimetre.

It's not unusual for the bridge to need positioning at a slight angle with the treble (E string) side nearer the fingerboard than the bass (G string) side. This is to compensate for the different thicknesses of the string windings.

Remember to slacken the strings before you move the bridge and tune them again to make more checks. This can be a very time consuming process, but once completed need only be repeated if the bridge is knocked or if all the strings are removed at the same time. Occasionally this will be necessary to give the fingerboard a good clean but if you change strings one at a time the bridge will remain held in position.

The action is too high

'Action' means the height of the strings from the fingerboard. If it's too high, deep gouges are cut in the left hand fingers and eventually rivers of blood will run down the fingerboard as you play *The Flight of the Bumblebee* for the umpteenth time.

If you play a round-back you will have to lower the bridge by drastic means: applying sandpaper, chisels and even chainsaws. This job is better left to a good repair person. If you play a flat-back have no fear! Most bridges on flat-backs have two tiny height adjustment wheels at either end. Slacken the strings, but not to the extent that the bridge moves, then roll the wheels until the bridge lowers. Tighten the strings up to pitch again and see how things feel. You may have to repeat this procedure a few times until you find that happy medium where the strings are easy to press down but don't buzz on the frets. When you've found a comfortable height repeat the tuning checks described above, as the bridge height can sometimes affect its positioning.

There's a rattle when I play

This is something you should check for when you buy the instrument, but with time wood shifts and settles, machine heads wear out and the mandolin starts suffering from pure old age. This is cause for rejoicing! Old instruments are like trusted old friends; they have a character, a warmth, a beauty of tone and a glorious patina that only old age can bring. But instruments are like people or cars; if they don't get a good service occasionally, they break down.

Rattles have a number of causes. Cheap machine heads won't last a lifetime (good ones will), and may wear loose and start to rattle. Hold each one in turn as you strum the open strings and see if the rattle stops. An elastic band stretched round the pegs can sometimes effect a temporary solution, but you may need to buy new ones.

If you think the rattle is coming from the tailpiece try wedging a small piece of leather or foam between the tailpiece and the body. You can try the same thing between the strings and the headstock if the rattle is coming from the other end of the instrument. None of these are very elegant remedies but they could get you out of bother in the short term.

If the body of the instrument is rattling this is more serious and may mean a crack or a loose strut inside in which case you should seek professional help.

GOOD-BYE

A guitarist friend once told me that sometimes when he's teaching he turns the guitar round and tries to play left-handed; this way, he can better appreciate what a beginner feels like trying to stretch fingers into some seemingly impossible position. For those of us who have been playing a few years it's a vivid reminder of how awkward it feels when you start, but even if you've been playing only a short time it can still be an interesting measure of how much progress you've made.

By now you should have reached the stage where the mandolin feels a comfortable and natural thing to hold. It's time to think beyond reaching the end of a tune without making mistakes. Somebody once quoted the four Ts as being the important factors in music making: technique, tone, taste and touch.

They're all important. Never forget that a good technique is a means to an artistic end, and the same is true of the ability to read music. But developing a good ear is something you should not neglect. If you hear a tune can you play it? Get a friend to play some simple phrases at you and see if you can play them straight back.

Tone is something you should think seriously about now that you've been playing a little while. Use a tape recorder and listen back to yourself; if you hear a thin, clicky sound with lots of plectrum noise start experimenting with your plectrum. I find that even though my plectrum stroke is at about 90° to the strings, if I *turn the plectrum* to about 45° the tone is thickened considerably. Many people fail to give any thought at all to their right hand in an all-out rush to develop a lightening-fast left hand, but they are equally important.

Taste is so subjective I won't dwell on it, but do try to exercise it.

Touch is the most important T. There are musicians who have only a basic technique yet manage to tug our heartstrings simply by the way they play. Now that you've grasped the basics of the mandolin think more of playing with colour, expression, dynamics and to make the music come to life in your own unique way. Use simple tunes so you don't have to think about the technical side of things. Touch is something that comes not from the printed page, not from the fingers or head, but from within you. Your individuality is your greatest asset.

Having all four Ts in abundance is a quality that distinguishes a great musician from a good one, but that's something to think about next week.

Good-bye until then.

More from Simon Mayor...

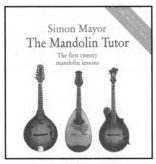

CDACS 028

The Mandolin Tutor (CD)

The essential accompaniment to this book!

Simon Mayor plays and talks you through all the material with guitar backing. Mandolin and guitar are heard in total stereo separation on your system, so you can play along to the accompaniment, hear solo mandolin, or both together.

'Should be an inspiration to all aspiring mandolin players. I could not fault this material in any way. It's way, way better than anything of this sort that I've seen.' Folk Roots

New Celtic Mandolin (DVD)

For those who already know their way round the mandolin and want some expert advice and new ideas to spice up their playing of Celtic music.

Simon Mayor takes a fresh and detailed look at five traditional and modern Celtic tunes, introducing original ideas and techniques that will benefit all aspects of mandolin playing.

Tunes covered include: The Dark and Slender Boy (Irish trad), Dance of the Waterboatmen (Mayor), Athol Highlanders (Scottish trad), The Butterfly (Irish trad), Waynesboro (New England trad)

DVACS 046

DVACS 045

Mandolin Essentials (DVD)

A learn-as-you-play approach for those in the early stages of mandolin playing.

Simon's informal and encouraging style gets you playing five easy tunes in a variety of musical idioms, taking a detailed look at left hand fingering, right hand techniques, tips for making simple tunes sound more interesting, and lots, lots more.

ISBN: 0-9522776-2-X

New Celtic Mandolin (book)

Thirty-one tunes from all corners of the Celtic World in standard notation and tablature with guitar chords.

Includes extensive technical guidance, three arrangements for quartet and interviews with top players Andy Irvine, Maartin Allcock, Chris Newman, Gary Peterson and Brian Taheny.

Includes tunes from Simon's 'New Celtic Mandolin' CD.

Mastering The Mandolin (book / CD)

A follow-on from The Mandolin Tutor book and CD.

Mastering The Mandolin is a detailed course for those who have already covered the basics of mandolin playing, incorporating closed position playing, position shifts, fourth finger workouts, chordal arrangements, bunched and extended fingerings, tremolo, double stopping and many tricks of the trade to help you on your way to mastering the mandolin.

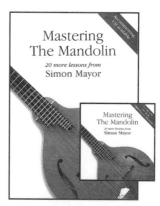

ISBN: 0952277638 / CDACS 044

ISBN: 0-9522776-0-3

The New Mandolin (book)

Simon Mayor's book of 21 tunes taken from across his first three mandolin albums is laced with technical tips and humorous anecdotes.

The music is presented in standard notation and tablature and this updated edition now includes examples of harmony lines and quartet arrangements.

Secure online ordering:
www.acousticsrecords.co.uk

CDACS 055

Music From A Small Island (CD)

A musical journey from Dorset via Simon's native Yorkshire to Scotland. This is Simon Mayor's first album not to include the word 'mandolin' in the title! While the mandolin family features strongly, his fiddle and guitar playing come to the fore in a collection of Scottish folk tunes.

'...folk record of the year... evocative virtuosity and (from Hilary James) faultless singing'
The Daily Telegraph

The English Mandolin (CD)

New settings and adaptations of classical and traditional pieces for mandolin ensemble (mandolins, mandolas and mandocellos). Includes works by Holst, Warlock, Purcell, Grainger and German.

'This is a delight, Simon Mayor's mandolin playing is without peer'
Folk Roots

'Sheer musical brilliance'   BBC World Service

CDACS 025

CDACS 056

Dance Of The Comedians (CD)

The Mandolinquents captured live at New Greenham Arts - Simon Mayor, Hilary James, Richard Collins and Gerald Garcia present over an hour of stunning playing and musical fun.

'If the test for any live album is whether it makes you wish you had been present, this sails through with distinction.'
Daily Telegraph

Mandolinquents (CD)

The debut album from the Mandolinquents. Everything from hot swing and ragtime instrumentals from the mandolin orchestras of the 1930s, Irving Berlin, Mozart, Ravel and Tchaikovsky to lively reels, beautiful traditional Irish airs and Chinese and Brazilian folk tunes.

'I can't help but be transfixed by the sheer brilliance of all the musicians and the exquisite vocals of Hilary James... this is a more than worthy contender for album of the year!'
Steppin' Out

CDACS 034

Music From A Small Island (CD)

CDACS 055

A musical journey from Dorset via Simon's native Yorkshire to Scotland. This is Simon Mayor's first album not to include the word 'mandolin' in the title! While the mandolin family features strongly, his fiddle and guitar playing come to the fore in a collection of Scottish folk tunes.

'...folk record of the year... evocative virtuosity and (from Hilary James) faultless singing'
The Daily Telegraph

The English Mandolin (CD)

CDACS 025

New settings and adaptations of classical and traditional pieces for mandolin ensemble (mandolins, mandolas and mandocellos). Includes works by Holst, Warlock, Purcell, Grainger and German.

'This is a delight, Simon Mayor's mandolin playing is without peer'
Folk Roots

'Sheer musical brilliance'   BBC World Service

Dance Of The Comedians (CD)

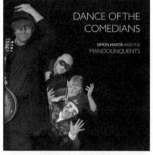

CDACS 056

The Mandolinquents captured live at New Greenham Arts - Simon Mayor, Hilary James, Richard Collins and Gerald Garcia present over an hour of stunning playing and musical fun.

'If the test for any live album is whether it makes you wish you had been present, this sails through with distinction.'
Daily Telegraph

Mandolinquents (CD)

CDACS 034

The debut album from the Mandolinquents. Everything from hot swing and ragtime instrumentals from the mandolin orchestras of the 1930s, Irving Berlin, Mozart, Ravel and Tchaikovsky to lively reels, beautiful traditional Irish airs and Chinese and Brazilian folk tunes.

'I can't help but be transfixed by the sheer brilliance of all the musicians and the exquisite vocals of Hilary James... this is a more than worthy contender for album of the year!'
Steppin' Out

Simon Mayor

If you would like up-to-date news of books, recordings
and concerts by Simon Mayor drop a line to Acoustics.

You can use the form below.

(feel free to photocopy it but please don't copy other pages).

Visit Simon Mayor's website:
www.mandolin.co.uk

secure ordering:
www.acousticsrecords.co.uk

Please keep me informed of future books, recordings
and concerts by Simon Mayor

Name ....

Address ....

....

....

Post (zip) code ....

Email ....

Acoustics Records, PO Box 350, Reading RG6 7DQ, England
Tel: +44 (0)118 926 8615   mail@acousticsrecords.co.uk
www.acousticsrecords.co.uk